Writing Grade 1 CD-3716   Printed in the United States of America   ISBN 0-88724-434-3

A NOTE TO PARENTS AND TEACHERS

Children are natural storytellers. Most of them can hardly wait to recount their experiences to their teacher or friends. An important task of the parent and teacher is to turn these storytellers into story writers. Children who begin to write early become comfortable with the process. Writing becomes as natural as speaking. It is important to make writing a part of the daily schedule.

Many children find writing difficult because they do not understand how to write. They do not even know how to begin. Any writing activity must be modeled by the teacher several times before a child can grasp the concepts. To achieve the greatest affect, the activity should be conducted with a group. This allows the free exchange of ideas and prompts deeper thinking that will assist in better clarity and comprehension of the concepts. When the task is fully understood and mastered within groups, individual assignments become appropriate.

Writing is a process, and it takes time to develop ideas into a finished product. Neither the teacher nor student should expect a well designed story to emerge from an initial attempt. Teachers and students should look upon writing as a five step process. The first step is gathering ideas pertaining to the writing assignment. The second step is selecting and organizing those ideas into a rough draft. Third is the revising step to reorganize content and refine wording. The fourth step is editing (proofreading) for grammar, capitalization, and punctuation errors. Lastly, the paper is rewritten as a final copy. Remember to use these five steps to guide the writing process.

Students do willingly what they do well. Direct instruction, ample opportunities to practice skills, and exciting topics will support these storytellers in our quest to make them story writers.

About the author...

During her many years as an educator, **Rae Anne Roberson** has taught in elementary, junior and senior high, and university level settings. She is currently the Title 1 Instructional Facilitator in her school system and is helping to develop several innovative reading programs for "at risk" students in elementary schools. Rae Anne is very active as a presenter at workshops for teachers and parents. She was recently presented with the "Award for Literacy" for her school system. Certified in elementary and secondary education as well as reading specialist, Rae Anne holds an M.Ed. and is currently working toward her doctorate.

Senior Editors: Patricia Pedigo and Roger DeSanti
Production Supervisor: Homer Desrochers
Production: Arlene Evitts and Debra Ollier

CD-3716

Ready-To-Use Ideas and Activities

The activities in this book will help students master the basic skills necessary to become competent writers. Remember as you read through the activities listed below, and as you go through this book, that all children learn at their own rate. Although repetition is important, it is critical that we never lose sight of the fact that it is equally important to build children's self-esteem and self-confidence if we want them to become successful learners as well as good citizens.

If you are working with a child at home, try to set up a quiet comfortable environment where you will work. Make it a special time to which you each look forward. Do only a few activities at a time. Try to end each session on a positive note, and remember that fostering self-esteem and self-confidence are also critical to the learning process.

The back of this book has removable flash cards that will be great for use for basic skill and vocabulary enrichment activities. Pull the flash cards out and either cut them apart or, if you have access to a paper cutter, use that to cut the flash cards apart.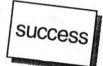

Explain the connection between the spoken and written word by asking a student to tell you what he or she did last weekend. Write the story on a large sheet of chart paper or on the chalkboard. point out the beginning, middle, and end of the story as well as the punctuation.

I had a fun weekend. My sister and I went to the zoo. We saw many different kinds of animals. My sister fed some of the animals. We had lunch and then we played on the slide. We went home at 3:00.

Ready-To-Use Ideas and Activities

Expose your students to the many types of writing that are out in the world. Newspapers, magazines, advertisements, weather forecasts, recipes, poems, automotive manuals, short stories, novels, personal letters, and more.

Each child will bring his or her own unique background and perspective to the writing task and will, therefore, produce unpredictable responses. However, each written task does require that certain elements be present for the exercise to be correctly completed. Application of guidelines below will be necessary for accurate grading or interpretation of the written responses.

There are two perspectives from which the adult may choose to assess written assignments: content and mechanics. Content assessment takes a look at what the child has written with a focus on the intended message. Mechanics assessment gives attention to capitalization, punctuation, indentation, spelling, grammar, and format of the written piece.

CONTENT ASSESSMENT CHECKLIST

Does the story follow a logical sequence?
Does the story stick to the topic?
Has the child incorporated the selected key words from the web or story box?
Are adjectives used appropriately to help describe the topic?
Does the story present a clear idea or theme?
Does the story have a beginning, middle and end?

MECHANICS ASSESSMENT CHECKLIST

Are capitals used at the beginning of each sentence?
Are capitals used for all proper nouns?
Has proper punctuation been used (periods or question marks)?
Is each paragraph indented?
Is a title included when appropriate?
Has the child used correct or inventive spellings?
Has the child printed legibly?
Has the assignment been completed in a manner consistent with the given format (sentence, paragraph, invitation, etc.)?

Ready-To-Use Ideas and Activities

Reproduce the bingo sheet included in this book, making enough to have one for each student. Hand them out to the students. Take the flash cards and write the words on the chalkboard. Have the students choose 24 of the words and write them in any order on the empty spaces of their bingo cards, writing only one word in each space. When all students have finished filling out their bingo cards, take the flash cards and make them in to a deck. Call out the words one at a time. Any student who has a called out word should make an "X" through the word to cross it out. The student who crosses out five words in a row first (horizontally, vertically, or diagonally) wins the game and shouts "BINGO!".

Reproduce this page and make your own bingo game! Use in conjunction with the enclosed flashcards.

B I N G O

		Free!		

Pick a sentence and write a story about it.

See my new shoes? I ...   Yellow leaves...   The school bus...

I am always...   Monday is...   Chocolate cake...

When I get out of bed...   September is when...

My best friend is...   Dad is always...

My book bag...   After school I...

Summer was...   Cats play...

Apples are...   Books are...

I run and...   Birds fly...

SEPTEMBER

_____

_____

_____

_____

_____

_____

_____

Name _____

Pick a sentence and write a story about it.

When I go trick-or-treating...   I like ...   I went to a party ...

My red jacket...   Two little cats...   The wind blows ...

I ride my bike ...   The witch rides...   October is...   Ghosts will...

Mom lets me ...   My friend and I ...   Tuesday we will...

Leaves fall...   The puppy ...   Pumpkins are...

I love to go ...

Pizza is ...

OCTOBER

Pick a sentence and write a story about it.

I can write ...   A squirrel in the tree ...   Turkey and potatoes ...

My class will ...   I cleaned ...   The trees...   The soccer ball...

Thanksgiving is ... Let's go outside and ...   Cold winds blow ...

I lost my hat. Now I ...   My new coat ...   The Pilgrims came ...

Thursday will be ...   Pumpkin pie is ...   Mom will cook ...

Grandma has...   It is time for ...

NOVEMBER

_____

_____

_____

_____

_____

_____

_____

Pick a sentence and write a story about it.

We went shopping for ...   My family ...   On Wednesday I ...

It is cold because ... I love to hear ...   I can hardly wait for ...

I would like to have ...   I will help Dad ...   In December we ...

I need a coat and ...   The lights are ...   Red and green...

Candy canes ...   We eat ...

I can bake ...

My sister ...

I saw ...

DECEMBER

Pick a sentence and write a story about it.

I like winter because...

We ride our sled ...

The gray sky ...

Two snowmen ...

Snowflakes fell ...

The night is ...

I can skate ...

I lost my ...

I have a new...

School is ...

JANUARY

Dad took me to ...

I like to watch ...

Every Friday ...

January is ...

It is cold ...

Pick a sentence and write a story about it.

The groundhog will ...   Roses are ...   I made a valentine for ...

The tooth fairy ...   The mother cat ...   The sad puppy ...

A big pink heart ...   Snow makes me ...   I am happy ...

I wish I could ...   Cookies are ...

FEBRUARY

February is ...   I found ...

I love ...   I always give ...

My job is ...   At recess ...

We need a hat for ...   My secret friend is ...

Name _____

Pick a sentence and write a story about it.

The leaves are ...   It is time to ...   Splash! The ...   March is ...

The birthday party was ...   Wear green because ...

I like to play ...   My pet is ...   Windy days ...   I can almost ...

My baby sister ...   Let's hide in the ...   Kites are flying ...

The ball game ...   **MARCH**   I cannot go to ...

Little birds ...   Last night I ...

_____

_____

_____

_____

_____

_____

_____

_____

7   CD-3716

Pick a sentence and write a story about it.

My umbrella ...   We hunt for ...   The rain in April ...

I will plant ...   Butterflies ...

I put a basket ...   White clouds ...

APRIL

_____

_____

_____

_____

_____

_____

I saw a frog ...   Flowers grow ...

The busy bee ...   Soft sunshine ...

The rainbow ...   The mother duck ...

Rain puddles are ...   Jumping rope ...

Let's go outside and ...   Some baby chicks ...

Pick a sentence and write a story about it.

I wrote a letter to ...   This summer I will ...   Show me how ...

A king wears ...   Airplanes... We picked ...   I know how to ...

Thank you for ...   I spilled ...   Hot dogs ...   The cowboy ...

Ladybugs ...   May is ...

Frogs ...   I want ...

MAY

_____
_____
_____
_____
_____
_____
_____

Pick a sentence and write a story about it.

This summer I ...   Summer will be ...   The water in the pool...

Let's build...   Last night I ...   My family...   The sun is ...

The hot sun ...   My skates ...   A black dog ...

I will go ...   The ants...   We sell ...   My house...   The bike...

JUNE

_____

_____

_____

_____

_____

_____

_____

_____

Horses ...   I like ...   Trees...   I can swim ...

In the summer...   My friend lives...   I like to visit ...

Name _____

| A sentence begins with a capital and ends with a period. |

Write each sentence using capitals and periods.

1. we have a new horse

_____

- -

_____

2. his name is Star

_____

- -

_____

3. star lives in the barn

_____

- -

_____

4. he likes to run fast

_____

- -

_____

5. he is my best friend

_____

- -

_____

Draw a picture of Star on the back of this page.

Nov.

Name _____

A sentence begins with a capital and ends with a period.

Write each sentence using capitals and periods.

1. my mother took me shopping

   _____

   -

   _____

2. i needed new shoes

   _____

   -

   _____

3. we looked in many stores

   _____

   -

   _____

4. we found some shoes

   _____

   -

   _____

5. i have them on

   _____

   -

   _____

Draw my new shoes on the back of this page.

| A sentence begins with a capital and ends with a period. |

Write each sentence using capitals and periods.

1. i ride the bus to school

_____

- -

_____

2. today the bus is late

_____

- -

_____

3. now i see it coming

_____

- -

_____

4. we must hurry

_____

- -

_____

5. we cannot miss school

_____

- -

_____

Draw a picture of the bus on the back of this page.

| A sentence begins with a capital and ends with a period. |

Write each sentence using capitals and periods.

1. i like the park

_____

- -

_____

2. i go every day

_____

- -

_____

3. i play ball with friends

_____

- -

_____

4. there are many flowers

_____

- -

_____

5. the park is fun

_____

- -

_____

Draw a picture of the park on the back of this page.

A sentence begins with a capital and ends with a period.

Write each sentence using capitals and periods.

1. today is my birthday

_____

- -

_____

2. i will have a party

_____

- -

_____

3. all my friends will come

_____

- -

_____

4. there will be a big cake

_____

- -

_____

5. i love birthdays

_____

- -

_____

Draw a picture of my cake on the back of this page.

Oct,

Name _____

| Every sentence has a beginning and an end. |

Match the beginnings and endings to make five sentences.

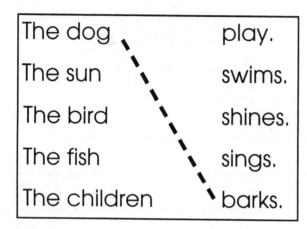

The dog	play.
The sun	swims.
The bird	shines.
The fish	sings.
The children	barks.

1. _____

2. _____

3. _____

4. _____

5. _____

Every sentence has a beginning and an end.

Match the beginnings and endings to make five sentences.

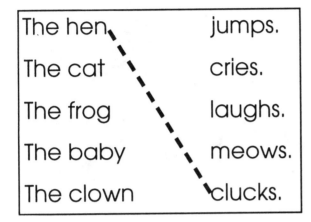

The hen	jumps.
The cat	cries.
The frog	laughs.
The baby	meows.
The clown	clucks.

1. _____

2. _____

3. _____

4. _____

5. _____

Every sentence has a beginning and an end.

Match the beginnings and endings to make five sentences.

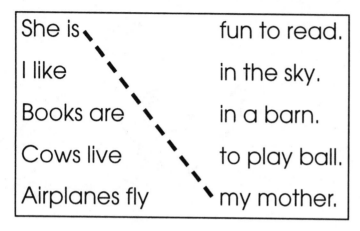

She is ⟍   fun to read.

I like   in the sky.

Books are   in a barn.

Cows live   to play ball.

Airplanes fly ⟍ my mother.

1. _____

2. _____

3. _____

4. _____

5. _____

Every sentence has a beginning and an end.

Match the beginnings and endings to make five sentences.

Show me how	some cake.
It is time	are big.
Some dinosaurs	to go home.
You may have	is red.
The color of fire	to ride a bike.

1. _____

2. _____

3. _____

4. _____

5. _____

Every sentence has a beginning and an end.

Match the beginnings and endings to make five sentences.

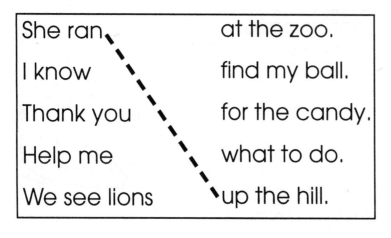

She ran	at the zoo.
I know	find my ball.
Thank you	for the candy.
Help me	what to do.
We see lions	up the hill.

1. _____

2. _____

3. _____

4. _____

5. _____

Every sentence has a beginning and an end.

Write the beginning of the sentence on the line.

| The leaves |
| Fall |
| The trees |
| Cold wind |
| Winter |

1. _____ comes after summer.

2. _____ turn pretty colors.

3. _____ blows the leaves.

4. _____ are bare.

5. _____ will be here soon.

| Every sentence has a beginning and an end. |

Write the beginning of the sentence on the line.

| Milk |
| Good food |
| Farm animals |
| We get |
| Hens |

1. _____ give us food.

2. _____ comes from cows.

3. _____ lay eggs.

4. _____ ham from pigs.

5. _____ helps us grow.

22 CD-3716

Every sentence has a beginning and an end.

Write the beginning of the sentence on the line.

Her house
It
My family
Grandma
A plane

1. _____ will visit Grandma.

2. _____ is far away.

3. _____ will take us there.

4. _____ will make cookies.

5. _____ will be nice to see her.

Name _____ Skill: Sentence Beginnings

| Every sentence has a beginning and an end. |

Write the beginning of the sentence on the line.

| Witches |
| Pumpkins |
| Today |
| Trick-or-treating |
| Ghosts |

_____

1. _____ is Halloween.

_____

2. _____ fly on brooms.

_____

3. _____say "boo" and laugh.

_____

4. _____ have yellow smiles.

_____

5. _____ will be lots of fun.

Every sentence has a beginning and an end.

Write the ending of the sentence on the line.

is Spot.

wags.

is brown and black.

play every day.

are big and floppy.

1. My puppy _____

2. His name _____

3. His tail always _____

4. His ears _____

5. We _____

Every sentence has a beginning and an end.

Write the ending of the sentence on the line.

> make a good dinner.
>
> come out of eggs.
>
> makes a nest.
>
> cry for food.
>
> is in a tree.

1. **Mother bird** _____

2. **The nest** _____

3. **Baby birds** _____

4. **They** _____

5. **Worms** _____

Every sentence has a beginning and an end.

Write the ending of the sentence on the line.

climb trees.
eat peanuts.
are at the zoo.
roar.
live here.

1. We _____

2. The monkeys _____

3. The lions _____

4. The elephants _____

5. Many animals _____

Every sentence has a beginning and an end.

Write the ending of the sentence on the line.

Dec

goes on my head.

will be warm.

go on my feet.

is cold outside.

go on my hands.

_____

1. It _____

_____

2. **Boots** _____

_____

3. **Mittens** _____

_____

4. **A hat** _____

_____

5. I _____

Every sentence has a beginning and an end.

Write the ending of the sentence on the line.

rolls out the door.
calls his kitten.
is time to rest.
play ball together.
comes to him.

1. Dan _____

2. The kitten _____

3. Dan and his kitten _____

4. The ball _____

5. It _____

Unscramble the words to make a sentence. Draw a picture about each sentence.

1	**2**
brown is dog My	dog My barks
3	**4**
ball plays He	dog My plays me with

Name _____

Unscramble the words to make a sentence. Draw a picture about each sentence.

1	**2**
funny She hat a has	green It is
- - - - - - - - - - - - - - - -	- - - - - - - - - - - - - - - -
- - - - - - - - - - - - - - - -	- - - - - - - - - - - - - - - -
3	**4**
will a ride horse Father	brown horse The is
- - - - - - - - - - - - - - - -	- - - - - - - - - - - - - - - -
- - - - - - - - - - - - - - - -	- - - - - - - - - - - - - - - -

Unscramble the words to make a sentence. Draw a picture about each sentence.

1

see I kittens three

2

The asleep are kittens

3

me Show bike your

4

race I bike my

Unscramble the words to make a sentence. Draw a picture about each sentence.

1	**2**
made cake a Mother	was The pretty cake
3	**4**
jumped frog The	was in It water the

Unscramble the words to make a sentence. Draw a picture about each sentence.

1 goes car fast This ------------------- -------------------	**2** It green a car is ------------------- -------------------
3 climb I tree the ------------------- -------------------	**4** orange has leaves It ------------------- -------------------

Name _____

Unscramble the words to make a sentence. Draw a picture about each sentence.

1	**2**
have We school at fun	to like I swing
3	**4**
reads book The a girl	book The big is

Unscramble the words to make a sentence. Draw a picture about each sentence.

1

away pig One ran

2

gate open The was

3

drink milk We chocolate

4

milk us Cows give.

Unscramble the words to make a sentence. Draw a picture about each sentence.

1	**2**
is pen in goat My a	goat My white is
3	**4**
apple red have I a	is Your green apple

Unscramble the words to make a sentence. Draw a picture about each sentence.

1	**2**
yellow is The duck	swims It pond in
3	**4**
boat paints Dad the	boat the I saw

Unscramble the words to make a sentence. Draw a picture about each sentence.

1 Come party my to	2 play We games will
3 can run I fast	4 won I ribbon a

A sentence tells a whole idea. It has a beginning and an end.

Find the spaces with a complete sentence. Color them brown. Color the other spaces yellow.

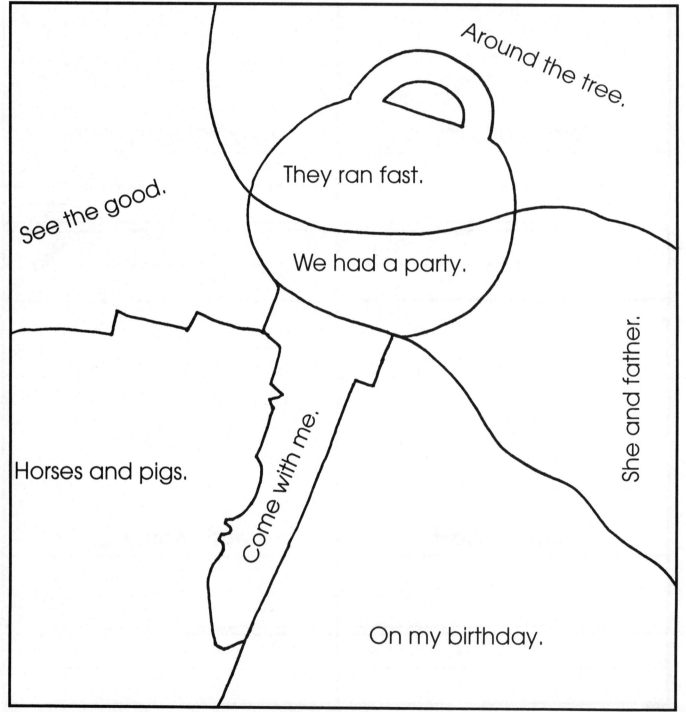

Around the tree.

They ran fast.

See the good.

We had a party.

She and father.

Horses and pigs.

Come with me.

On my birthday.

A sentence tells a whole idea. It has a beginning and an end.

**Find the spaces with a complete sentence. Color them red.
Color the other spaces green.**

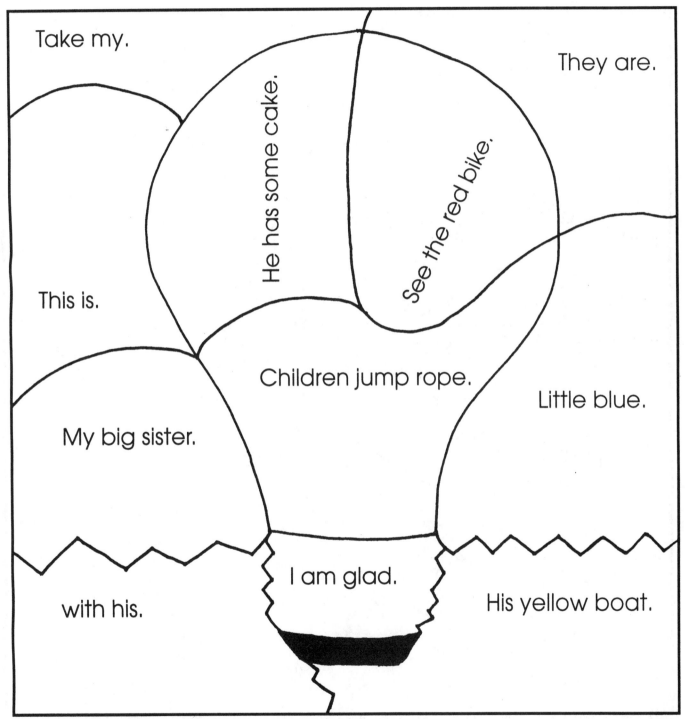

Take my.

They are.

He has some cake.

See the red bike.

This is.

Children jump rope.

Little blue.

My big sister.

I am glad.

with his.

His yellow boat.

Name _____

A sentence tells a whole idea. It has a beginning and an end.

Find the spaces with a complete sentence. Color them green. Color the other spaces orange.

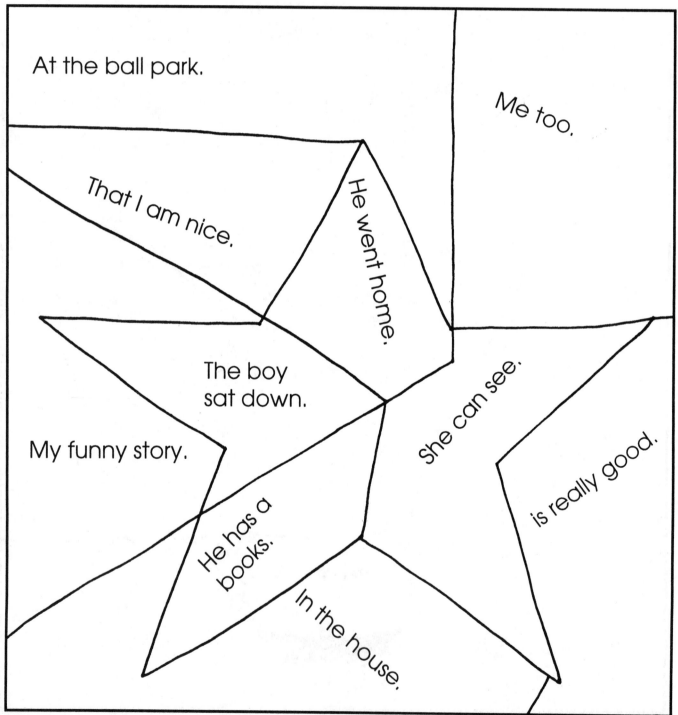

At the ball park.

Me too.

That I am nice.

He went home.

The boy sat down.

She can see.

My funny story.

is really good.

He has a books.

In the house.

42   CD-3716

A sentence tells a whole idea. It has a beginning and an end.

Find the spaces with a complete sentence. Color them yellow. Color the other spaces black.

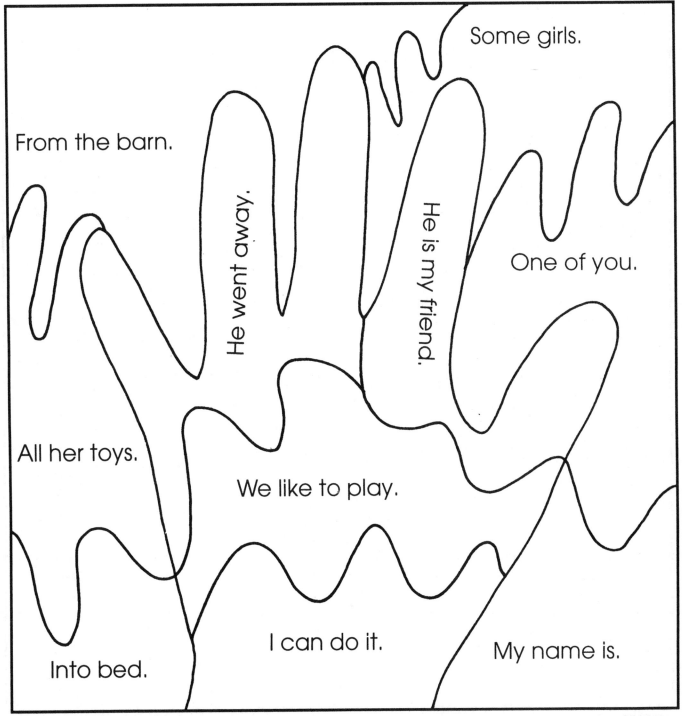

Some girls.

From the barn.

He went away.

He is my friend.

One of you.

All her toys.

We like to play.

I can do it.

Into bed.

My name is.

A sentence tells a whole idea. It has a beginning and an end.

**Find the spaces with a complete sentence. Color them red.
Color the other spaces purple.**

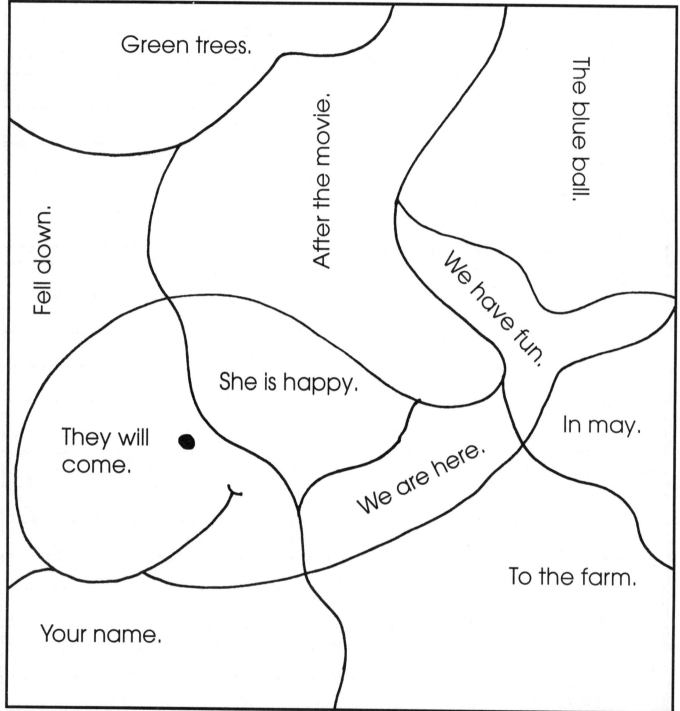

A sentence tells a whole idea. It has a beginning and an end.

Write a sentence about each picture. Make the first letter a capital. End with a period. Color the picture.

1.

balloon

2.

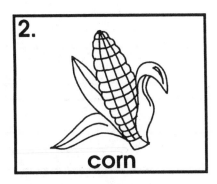

corn

3.

milk

4.

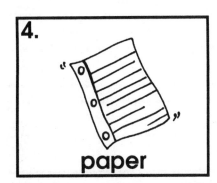

paper

A sentence tells a whole idea. It has a beginning and an end.

Write a sentence about each picture. Make the first letter a capital. End with a period. Color the picture.

1.
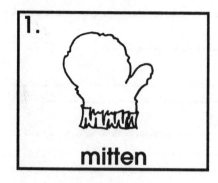
mitten

_____
- -
_____
_____
- -

2.
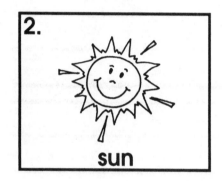
sun

_____
- -
_____
_____
- -
_____

3.

pig

_____
- -
_____
_____
- -

4.

baby

_____
- -
_____
_____
- -
_____

A sentence tells a whole idea. It has a beginning and an end.

Write a sentence about each picture. Make the first letter a capital. End with a period. Color the picture.

1. leaf

_____
- -
_____
_____
- -

2. kite

_____
- -
_____
_____
- -

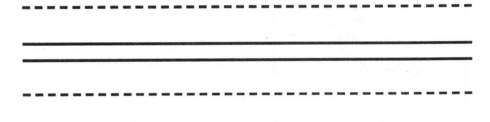

3. boat

_____
- -
_____
_____
- -

4. frog

_____
- -
_____
_____
- -

A sentence tells a whole idea. It has a beginning and an end.

Write a sentence about each picture. Make the first letter a capital. End with a period. Color the picture.

1.

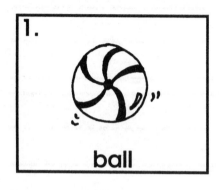

ball

_____

- -

_____

- -

_____

2.

cup

_____

- -

_____

- -

_____

3.

bee

_____

- -

_____

- -

_____

4.

coat

_____

- -

_____

- -

_____

Name _____

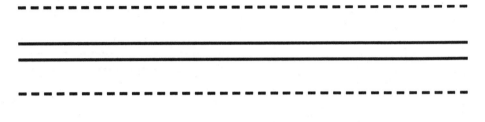

A sentence tells a whole idea. It has a beginning and an end.

Write a sentence about each picture. Make the first letter a capital. End with a period. Color the picture.

1. bird

2. flower

3. train

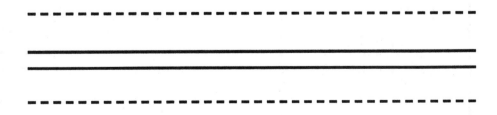

4. window

Name _____

A sentence tells a whole idea. It has a beginning and an end.

Write a sentence about each picture. Make the first letter a capital. End with a period. Color the picture.

1.

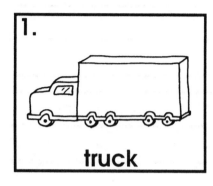

truck

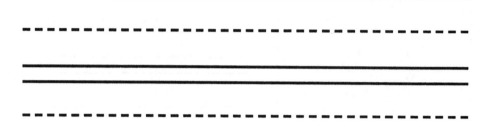

2.

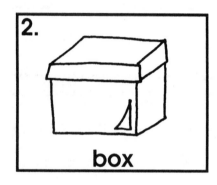

box

3.

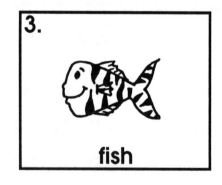

fish

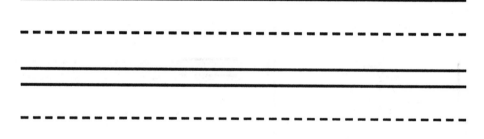

4.

turtle

50   CD-3716

A sentence tells a whole idea. It has a beginning and an end.

Write a sentence about each picture. Make the first letter a capital. End with a period. Color the picture.

1.

car

_____
- - - - - - - - - - - - - - - - - -
_____
- - - - - - - - - - - - - - - - - -
_____

2.

bear

- - - - - - - - - - - - - - - - - -
_____
- - - - - - - - - - - - - - - - - -
_____

3.
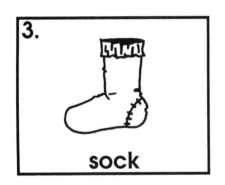
sock

- - - - - - - - - - - - - - - - - -
_____
- - - - - - - - - - - - - - - - - -
_____

4.

duck

- - - - - - - - - - - - - - - - - -
_____
- - - - - - - - - - - - - - - - - -
_____

A sentence tells a whole idea. It has a beginning and an end.

Write a sentence about each picture. Make the first letter a capital. End with a period. Color the picture.

1.
rabbit

2.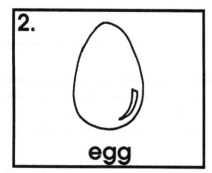
egg

3.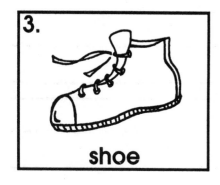
shoe

4.
goat

A sentence tells a whole idea. It has a beginning and an end.

Write a sentence about each picture. Make the first letter a capital. End with a period. Color the picture.

1.
farm

_____

- -

_____

- -

2.
dress

- -

_____

- -

_____

3.
clown

- -

_____

- -

4.
fire

- -

_____

- -

A sentence tells a whole idea. It has a beginning and an end.

Write a sentence about each picture. Make the first letter a capital. End with a period. Color the picture.

1.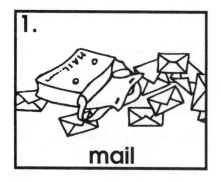
mail

_____

- -

_____

_____

- -

_____

2.
dog

_____

- -

_____

_____

- -

_____

3.
snake

_____

- -

_____

_____

- -

_____

4.
cat

_____

- -

_____

_____

- -

Name _____

A sentence that tells us something is called a statement.
A statement ends with a period.

Write two statements about each picture. Remember to use capitals and periods.

_____
- -
_____
- -
_____

_____
- -
_____
- -

Name _____

Skill: Writing Statements

A sentence that tells us something is called a statement.
A statement ends with a period.

Write two statements about each picture. Remember to use capitals and periods.

_____

- -

_____

- -

_____

_____

- -

_____

- -

A sentence that tells us something is called a statement.
A statement ends with a period.

Write two statements about each picture. Remember to use capitals and periods.

_____

- -

_____

- -

_____

_____

- -

_____

- -

Name _____

A sentence that tells us something is called a statement.
A statement ends with a period.

Write two statements about each picture. Remember to use capitals and periods.

A sentence that tells us something is called a statement.
A statement ends with a period.

Write two statements about each picture. Remember to use capitals and periods.

_____

- -

_____
_____

- -

_____

_____

- -

_____
_____

- -

A sentence that tells us something is called a statement.
A statement ends with a period.

Write two statements about each picture. Remember to use capitals and periods.

A sentence that tells us something is called a statement.
A statement ends with a period.

Write two statements about each picture. Remember to use capitals and periods.

A sentence that tells us something is called a statement.
A statement ends with a period.

Write two statements about each picture. Remember to use capitals and periods.

A sentence that tells us something is called a statement.
A statement ends with a period.

Write two statements about each picture. Remember to use capitals and periods.

A sentence that tells us something is called a statement.
A statement ends with a period.

Write two statements about each picture. Remember to use capitals and periods.

_____

- -

_____

- -

_____

_____

- -

_____

- -

Unscramble the words to make a question. Draw a picture about each question.

1

Are friend my you

- - - - - - - - - - - - - -

2

like you Do school

- - - - - - - - - - - - - -

3

name is What your

- - - - - - - - - - - - - -

4

wants Who to song a sing

- - - - - - - - - - - - - -

Name _____

Unscramble the words to make a question. Draw a picture about each question.

1 girl is that Who - - - - - - - - - - - - - - - - - - - - - - - - - - - - - - - - - -	**2** you book What will read - - - - - - - - - - - - - - - - - - - - - - - - - - - - - - - - - -
3 my boat Where is - - - - - - - - - - - - - - - - - - - - - - - - - - - - - - - - - -	**4** can When sing we - - - - - - - - - - - - - - - - - - - - - - - - - - - - - - - - - -

Unscramble the words to make a question. Draw a picture about each question.

1

blue sky Why the is

- -

- -

2

How you old are

- -

- -

3

that Is ball your

- -

- -

4

high Can jump she

- -

- -

Unscramble the words to make a question. Draw a picture about each question.

1	**2**
a you bike have Do	my these shoes Are
3	**4**
that dog Is your	like to frogs you Do eat

Unscramble the words to make a question. Draw a picture about each question.

1	**2**
boots Where your are	What sun color the is
3	**4**
school to go Why you do	Who best is friend your

Unscramble the words to make a question. Draw a picture about each question.

1	**2**
father home at your Is	shoes Are these red your
3	**4**
car new have you Do a	her see you did When

An asking sentence is a question. It ends with a question mark. Who, what, when, where, why, and how are some words that questions begin with.

Write a question about each picture. Remember to use capitals and question marks.

1.

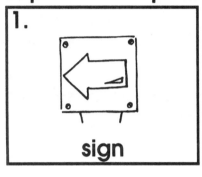

sign

2.

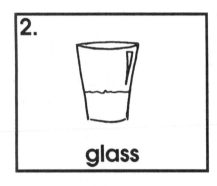

glass

3.

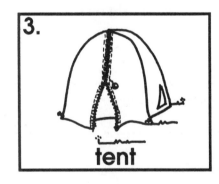

tent

4.

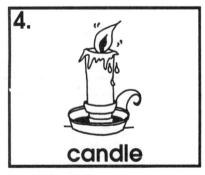

candle

An asking sentence is a question. It ends with a question mark. Who, what, when, where, why, and how are some words that questions begin with.

Write a question about each picture. Remember to use capitals and question marks.

1.

lamp

_____

_____

_____

2.
sock

_____

_____

_____

3.
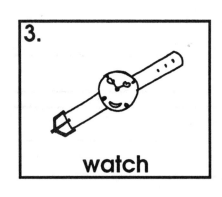
watch

_____

_____

_____

4.
hat

_____

_____

_____

An asking sentence is a question. It ends with a question mark. Who, what, when, where, why, and how are some words that questions begin with.

Write a question about each picture. Remember to use capitals and question marks.

1.
pot

2.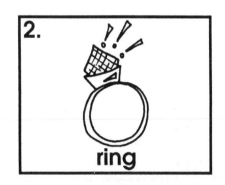
ring

3.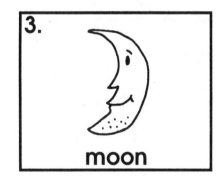
moon

4.
teacher

Name _____

An asking sentence is a question. It ends with a question mark. Who, what, when, where, why, and how are some words that questions begin with.

Write a question about each picture. Remember to use capitals and question marks.

1.
king

_____

- -

_____

- -

2.
cake

_____

- -

_____

- -

3.
jar

_____

- -

_____

- -

4.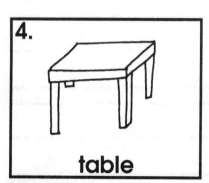
table

_____

- -

_____

- -

An asking sentence is a question. It ends with a question mark. Who, what, when, where, why, and how are some words that questions begin with.

Write a question about each picture. Remember to use capitals and question marks.

1.

mop

- -

_____

- -

2.
wagon

_____

- -

_____

- -

3.
sled

- -

_____

- -

4.
plant

_____

- -

_____

- -

An asking sentence is a question. It ends with a question mark. Who, what, when, where, why, and how are some words that questions begin with.

Write a question about each picture. Remember to use capitals and question marks.

1.
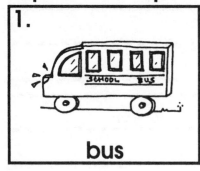
bus

_ _

_ _

2.

star

_ _

_ _

3.

duck

_ _

_ _

4.
coat

_ _

_ _

Name _____

An asking sentence is a question. It ends with a question mark. Who, what, when, where, why, and how are some words that questions begin with.

Write a question about each picture. Remember to use capitals and question marks.

1.
doll

_____

- - - - - - - - - - - - - - - - - - -

_____

- - - - - - - - - - - - - - - - - - -

_____

2.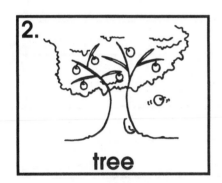
tree

_____

- - - - - - - - - - - - - - - - - - -

_____

- - - - - - - - - - - - - - - - - - -

_____

3.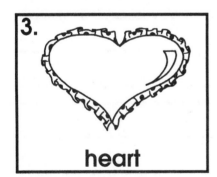
heart

_____

- - - - - - - - - - - - - - - - - - -

_____

- - - - - - - - - - - - - - - - - - -

_____

4.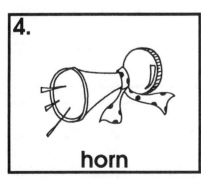
horn

_____

- - - - - - - - - - - - - - - - - - -

_____

- - - - - - - - - - - - - - - - - - -

_____

An asking sentence is a question. It ends with a question mark. Who, what, when, where, why, and how are some words that questions begin with.

Write a question about each picture. Remember to use capitals and question marks.

1.
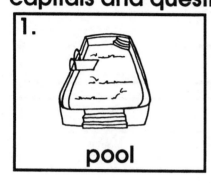
pool

2.
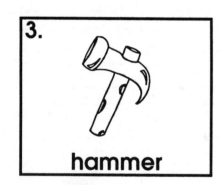
rain

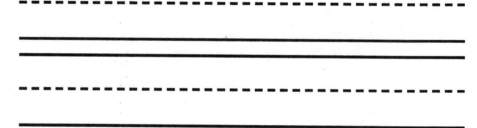

3.
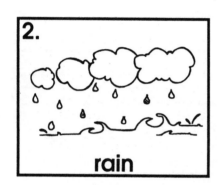
hammer

4.

clouds

These mixed up sentences tell a story. Write the sentences in order on the lines below. Remember to use capitals and periods. Draw a picture for the story.

Making a Cake

1. She put the pan into the oven.

2. Ellen mixed the cake batter.

3. Ellen ate a big piece of the cake.

1. _____

_____

2. _____

_____

3. _____

_____

These mixed up sentences tell a story. Write the sentences in order on the lines below. Remember to use capitals and periods. Draw a picture for the story.

Doing Laundry

1. You then fold the clothes neatly.

2. First, you wash the clothes.

3. Last, you put the clothes away.

1.

2.

3.

These mixed up sentences tell a story. Write the sentences in order on the lines below. Remember to use capitals and periods. Draw a picture for the story.

Get Ready!

1. Joshua went to school.

2. He ate a good breakfast.

3. Joshua jumped out of bed.

1.

2.

3.

These mixed up sentences tell a story. Write the sentences in order on the lines below. Remember to use capitals and periods. Draw a picture for the story.

Painting

1. Meyer took out some paper and paint.
2. Meyer gave the picture to his mom.
3. He painted a pretty picture of a flower.

1. _____

_____

2. _____

_____

3. _____

_____

These mixed up sentences tell a story. Write the sentences in order on the lines below. Remember to use capitals and periods. Draw a picture for the story.

The Rabbit

1. The rabbit hopped down a hole near the bush.
2. A rabbit sat under a bush in my yard.
3. I tried to catch the rabbit.

1.

2.

3.

Write a story about the picture. Use the words in the word box. Remember to begin each sentence with a capital letter and to end it with a period or question mark.

Word Box

puppy

black

lost

home

Write a story about the picture. Use the words in the word box. Remember to begin each sentence with a capital letter and to end it with a period or question mark.

Word Box
plane
fly
high
clouds

Name _____

Write a story about the picture. Use the words in the word box. Remember to begin each sentence with a capital letter and to end it with a period or question mark.

Word Box
squirrel
brown
nuts
winter

Write a story about the picture. Use the words in the word box. Remember to begin each sentence with a capital letter and to end it with a period or question mark.

Word Box
gray
elephant
trunk
peanuts

_____

- -

_____

- -

_____

- -

_____

- -

_____

- -

_____

- -

_____

Write a story about the picture. Use the words in the word box. Remember to begin each sentence with a capital letter and to end it with a period or question mark.

Word Box
petals
flower
yellow
bee

_____

- -

_____

_____

- -

_____

_____

- -

_____

_____

- -

_____

_____

- -

_____

Name _____

Write a story about the picture. Use the words in the word box. Remember to begin each sentence with a capital letter and to end it with a period or question mark.

Word Box
hide
game
friends
count

_____

- -

_____

- -

_____

- -

_____

- -

_____

- -

_____

Write a story about the picture. Use the words in the word box. Remember to begin each sentence with a capital letter and to end it with a period or question mark.

Word Box
storm
clouds
rain
wet

Write a story about the picture. Use the words in the word box. Remember to begin each sentence with a capital letter and to end it with a period or question mark.

Word Box
seal
water
ball
swim

Skill: Writing Stories

Write three more words about the picture in the word box. Use the words to write a story about the picture. Remember to begin each sentence with a capital letter.

Word Box
paint
_____
_____
_____

Write three more words about the picture in the word box.
Use the words to write a story about the picture. Remember
to begin each sentence with a capital letter.

Word Box
kite
_____
_____
_____

Write three more words about the picture in the word box. Use the words to write a story about the picture. Remember to begin each sentence with a capital letter.

Word Box
bake
_____
_____
_____

Write three more words about the picture in the word box.
Use the words to write a story about the picture. Remember
to begin each sentence with a capital letter.

Word Box
music
_____
_____
_____

_____

_____

_____

_____

_____

_____

_____

_____

_____

_____

_____

_____

_____

_____

_____

_____

Write three more words about the picture in the word box. Use the words to write a story about the picture. Remember to begin each sentence with a capital letter.

Word Box
swim
_____
_____
_____

Write three more words about the picture in the word box.
Use the words to write a story about the picture. Remember
to begin each sentence with a capital letter.

Word Box
chicken
_____
_____
_____

Write three more words about the picture in the word box.
Use the words to write a story about the picture. Remember
to begin each sentence with a capital letter.

Word Box
asleep
_____
_____
_____

**Write three more words about the picture in the word box.
Use the words to write a story about the picture. Remember
to begin each sentence with a capital letter.**

Word Box

ball

_____

_____

_____

_____

- -

_____

- -

_____

- -

_____

- -

_____

- -

_____

- -

_____

Write three more words about the picture in the word box. Use the words to write a story about the picture. Remember to begin each sentence with a capital letter.

Word Box

bus

_____

_____

_____

Writing Award

_____

receives this award for

_____

Keep up the great work!

_____ _____
signed   date

Writing Whiz!

_____

receives this award for

_____

Great Job!

_____ _____
signed   date

Wonderful Writing!

_____

receives this award for

_____

Keep up the great work!

_____ _____

signed   date

All Star Writer

_____

is a Writing All Star!

_____

You are terrific!

_____ _____

signed   date

Answer Key

Name _____ Skill: Creative Writing-September

Pick a sentence and write a story about it.

See my new shoes? I ...   Yellow leaves...   The school bus...

I am always... Monday is... Chocolate cake...

When I get out of bed...   September is when...

My best friend is...   Dad is always...

My book bag...   After school I...

Summer was...   Cats play...

Apples are...   Books are...

I run and...   **SEPTEMBER**   Birds fly...

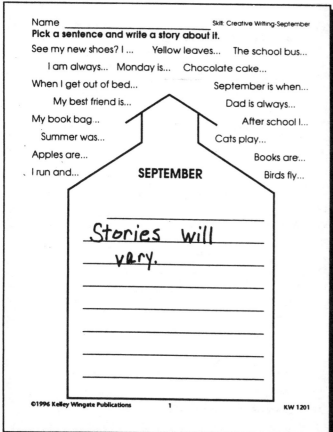

Stories will vary.

©1996 Kelley Wingate Publications   1   KW 1201

Name _____ Skill: Creative Writing-October

Pick a sentence and write a story about it.

When I go trick-or-treating...   I like ...   I went to a party ...

My red jacket...   Two little cats...   The wind blows ...

I ride my bike ... The witch rides... October is... Ghosts will...

Mom lets me ...   My friend and I ...   Tuesday we will...

Leaves fall...   The puppy ...   Pumpkins are...

I love to go ...   Pizza is ...

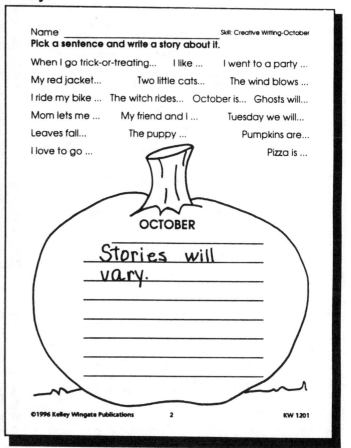

OCTOBER

Stories will vary.

©1996 Kelley Wingate Publications   2   KW 1201

Name _____ Skill: Creative Writing-November

Pick a sentence and write a story about it.

I can write ...   A squirrel in the tree ...   Turkey and potatoes ...

My class will ... I cleaned ...   The trees...   The soccer ball...

Thanksgiving is ... Let's go outside and ...   Cold winds blow ...

I lost my hat. Now I ...   My new coat ...   The Pilgrims came ...

Thursday will be ...   Pumpkin pie is ...   Mom will cook ...

Grandma has...   It is time for ...

NOVEMBER

Stories will vary.

©1996 Kelley Wingate Publications   3   KW 1201

Name _____ Skill: Creative Writing-December

Pick a sentence and write a story about it.

We went shopping for ...   My family ...   On Wednesday I ...

It is cold because ... I love to hear ...   I can hardly wait for ...

I would like to have ...   I will help Dad ...   In December we ...

I need a coat and ...   The lights are ...   Red and green...

Candy canes ...   We eat ...

I can bake ...

My sister ...

I saw ...

DECEMBER

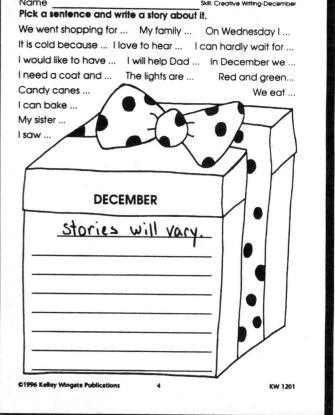

Stories will vary.

©1996 Kelley Wingate Publications   4   KW 1201

Name _____   Skill: Creative Writing-January
Pick a sentence and write a story about it.

I like winter because...   JANUARY   Dad took me to ...
We ride our sled ...   I like to watch ...
The gray sky ...   Every Friday ...
Two snowmen ...   January is ...
Snowflakes fell ...   It is cold ...
The night is ...
I can skate ...
I lost my ...
I have a new...
School is ...

Stories will vary.

©1996 Kelley Wingate Publications   5   KW 1201

Name _____   Skill: Creative Writing-February
Pick a sentence and write a story about it.

The groundhog will ...   Roses are ...   I made a valentine for ...
The tooth fairy ...   The mother cat ...   The sad puppy ...
A big pink heart ...   Snow makes me ...   I am happy ...
I wish I could ...   Cookies are ...

FEBRUARY

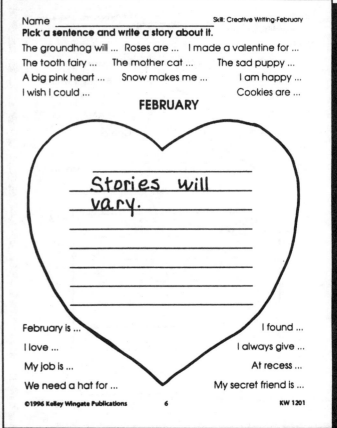

Stories will vary.

February is ...   I found ...
I love ...   I always give ...
My job is ...   At recess ...
We need a hat for ...   My secret friend is ...

©1996 Kelley Wingate Publications   6   KW 1201

Name _____   Skill: Creative Writing-March
Pick a sentence and write a story about it.

The leaves are ...   It is time to ...   Splash! The ...   March is ...
The birthday party was ...   Wear green because ...
I like to play ...   My pet is ...   Windy days ...   I can almost ...
My baby sister ...   Let's hide in the ...   Kites are flying ...
The ball game ...   **MARCH**   I cannot go to ...
Little birds ...   Last night I ...

Stories will vary.

©1996 Kelley Wingate Publications   7   KW 1201

Name _____   Skill: Creative Writing-April
Pick a sentence and write a story about it.

My umbrella ...   We hunt for ...   The rain in April ...
I will plant ...   Butterflies ...
I put a basket ...   White clouds ...

APRIL

Stories will vary.

I saw a frog ...   Flowers grow ...
The busy bee ...   Soft sunshine ...
The rainbow ...   The mother duck ...
Rain puddles are ...   Jumping rope ...
Let's go outside and ...   Some baby chicks ...

©1996 Kelley Wingate Publications   8   KW 1201

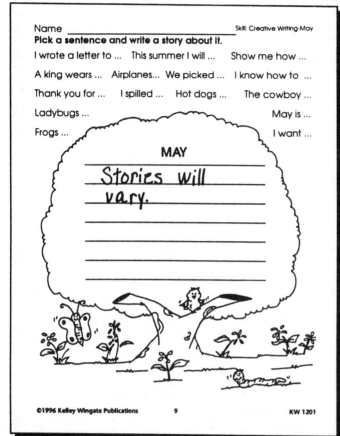

Name _____   Skill: Creative Writing-May
Pick a sentence and write a story about it.

I wrote a letter to ...   This summer I will ...   Show me how ...

A king wears ...   Airplanes...   We picked ...   I know how to ...

Thank you for ...   I spilled ...   Hot dogs ...   The cowboy ...

Ladybugs ...   May is ...

Frogs ...   I want ...

MAY

Stories will vary.

©1996 Kelley Wingate Publications   9   KW 1201

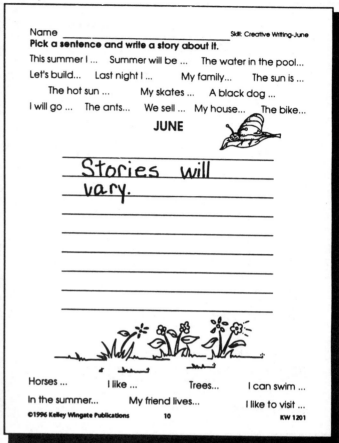

Name _____   Skill: Creative Writing-June
Pick a sentence and write a story about it.

This summer I ...   Summer will be ...   The water in the pool...

Let's build...   Last night I ...   My family...   The sun is ...

The hot sun ...   My skates ...   A black dog ...

I will go ...   The ants...   We sell ...   My house...   The bike...

JUNE

Stories will vary.

Horses ...   I like ...   Trees...   I can swim ...

In the summer...   My friend lives...   I like to visit ...

©1996 Kelley Wingate Publications   10   KW 1201

Name _____   Skill: Capitals and Periods

| A sentence begins with a capital and ends with a period. |

Write each sentence using capitals and periods.

1. we have a new horse

We have a new horse.

2. his name is Star

His name is Star.

3. star lives in the barn

Star lives in the barn.

4. he likes to run fast

He likes to run fast.

5. he is my best friend

He is my best friend.

Draw a picture of Star on the back of this page.

©1996 Kelley Wingate Publications   11   KW 1201

Name _____   Skill: Capitals and Periods

| A sentence begins with a capital and ends with a period. |

Write each sentence using capitals and periods.

1. my mother took me shopping

My mother took me shopping.

2. i needed new shoes

I needed new shoes.

3. we looked in many stores

We looked in many stores.

4. we found some shoes

We found some shoes.

5. i have them on

I have them on.

Draw my new shoes on the back of this page.

©1996 Kelley Wingate Publications   12   KW 1201

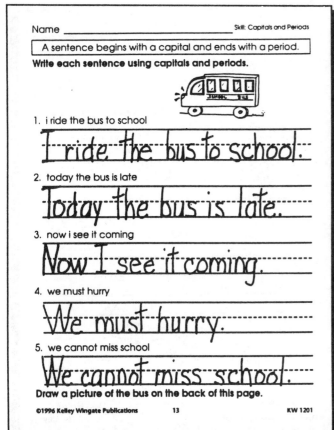

Name _____   Skill: Capitals and Periods

| A sentence begins with a capital and ends with a period. |

Write each sentence using capitals and periods.

1. i ride the bus to school

I ride the bus to school.

2. today the bus is late

Today the bus is late.

3. now i see it coming

Now I see it coming.

4. we must hurry

We must hurry.

5. we cannot miss school

We cannot miss school.

Draw a picture of the bus on the back of this page.

13

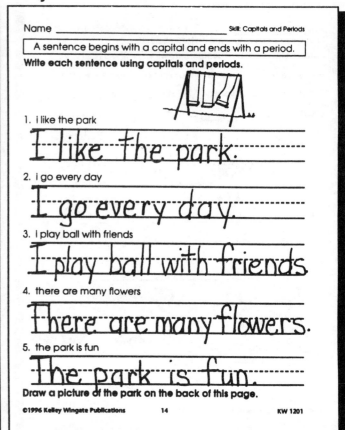

Name _____   Skill: Capitals and Periods

| A sentence begins with a capital and ends with a period. |

Write each sentence using capitals and periods.

1. i like the park

I like the park.

2. i go every day

I go every day.

3. i play ball with friends

I play ball with friends

4. there are many flowers

There are many flowers.

5. the park is fun

The park is fun.

Draw a picture of the park on the back of this page.

14

Name _____   Skill: Capitals and Periods

| A sentence begins with a capital and ends with a period. |

Write each sentence using capitals and periods.

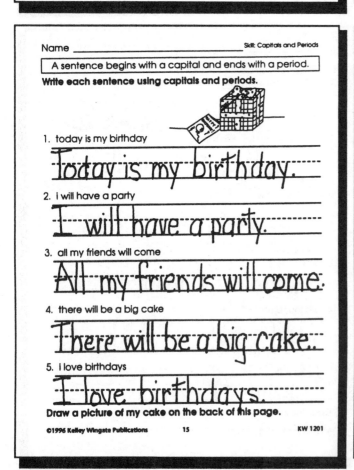

1. today is my birthday

Today is my birthday.

2. i will have a party

I will have a party.

3. all my friends will come

All my friends will come.

4. there will be a big cake

There will be a big cake.

5. i love birthdays

I love birthdays.

Draw a picture of my cake on the back of this page.

15

Name _____   Skill: Forming Sentences

| Every sentence has a beginning and an end. |

Match the beginnings and endings to make five sentences.

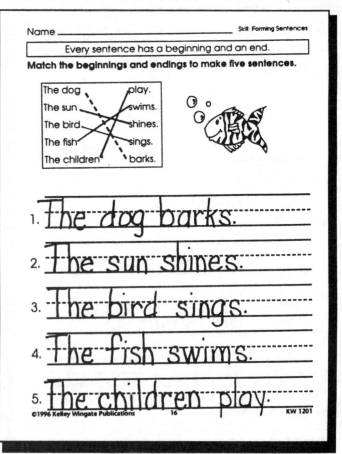

The dog   play.
The sun   swims.
The bird   shines.
The fish   sings.
The children   barks.

1. The dog barks.

2. The sun shines.

3. The bird sings.

4. The fish swims.

5. The children play.

16

Worksheet 1 (page 17)

Name _____   Skill: Forming Sentences

Every sentence has a beginning and an end.

Match the beginnings and endings to make five sentences.

The hen	jumps.
The cat	cries.
The frog	laughs.
The baby	meows.
The clown	clucks.

1. The hen clucks.
2. The cat meows.
3. The frog jumps.
4. The baby cries.
5. The clown laughs.

©1996 Kelley Wingate Publications   17   KW 1201

Worksheet 2 (page 18)

Name _____   Skill: Forming Sentences

Every sentence has a beginning and an end.

Match the beginnings and endings to make five sentences.

She is	fun to read.
I like	in the sky.
Books are	in a barn.
Cows live	to play ball.
Airplanes fly	my mother.

1. She is my mother.
2. I like to play ball.
3. Cows live in a barn.
4. Books are fun to read.
5. Airplanes fly in the sky.

©1996 Kelley Wingate Publications   18   KW 1201

Worksheet 3 (page 19)

Name _____   Skill: Forming Sentences

Every sentence has a beginning and an end.

Match the beginnings and endings to make five sentences.

Show me how	some cake.
It is time	are big.
Some dinosaurs	to go home.
You may have	is red.
The color of fire	to ride a bike.

1. Show me how to ride a bike.
2. It is time to go home.
3. Some dinosaurs are big.
4. You may have some cake.
5. The color of fire is red.

©1996 Kelley Wingate Publications   19   KW 1201

Worksheet 4 (page 20)

Name _____   Skill: Forming Sentences

Every sentence has a beginning and an end.

Match the beginnings and endings to make five sentences.

She ran	at the zoo.
I know	find my ball.
Thank you	for the candy.
Help me	what to do.
We see lions	up the hill.

1. She ran up the hill.
2. I know what to do.
3. Thank you for the candy.
4. Help me find my ball.
5. We see lions at the zoo.

©1996 Kelley Wingate Publications   20   KW 1201

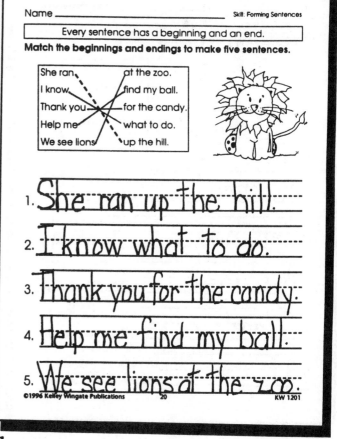

Answer Key

Name _____ Skill: Sentence Beginnings

| Every sentence has a beginning and an end. |

Write the beginning of the sentence on the line.

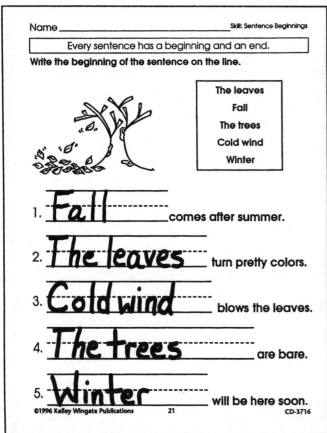

> The leaves
> Fall
> The trees
> Cold wind
> Winter

1. **Fall** comes after summer.

2. **The leaves** turn pretty colors.

3. **Cold wind** blows the leaves.

4. **The trees** are bare.

5. **Winter** will be here soon.

©1996 Kelley Wingate Publications   21   CD-3716

Name _____ Skill: Sentence Beginnings

| Every sentence has a beginning and an end. |

Write the beginning of the sentence on the line.

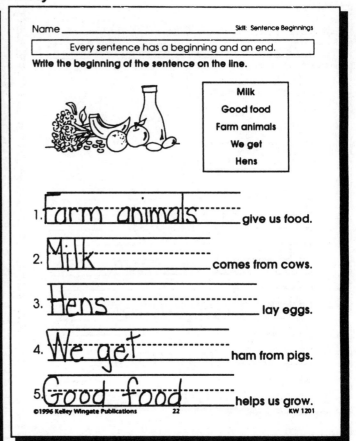

> Milk
> Good food
> Farm animals
> We get
> Hens

1. **Farm animals** give us food.

2. **Milk** comes from cows.

3. **Hens** lay eggs.

4. **We get** ham from pigs.

5. **Good food** helps us grow.

©1996 Kelley Wingate Publications   22   KW 1201

Name _____ Skill: Sentence Beginnings

| Every sentence has a beginning and an end. |

Write the beginning of the sentence on the line.

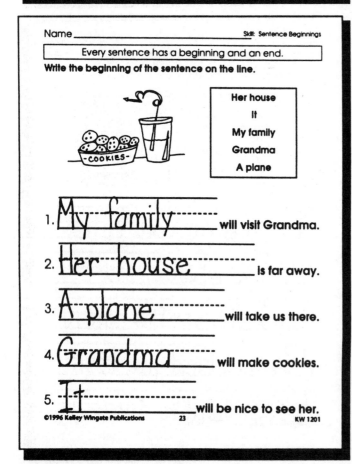

> Her house
> It
> My family
> Grandma
> A plane

1. **My family** will visit Grandma.

2. **Her house** is far away.

3. **A plane** will take us there.

4. **Grandma** will make cookies.

5. **It** will be nice to see her.

©1996 Kelley Wingate Publications   23   KW 1201

Name _____ Skill: Sentence Beginnings

| Every sentence has a beginning and an end. |

Write the beginning of the sentence on the line.

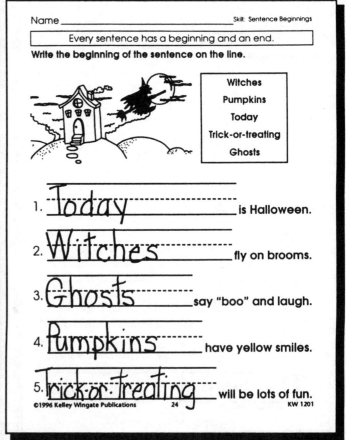

> Witches
> Pumpkins
> Today
> Trick-or-treating
> Ghosts

1. **Today** is Halloween.

2. **Witches** fly on brooms.

3. **Ghosts** say "boo" and laugh.

4. **Pumpkins** have yellow smiles.

5. **Trick-or-treating** will be lots of fun.

©1996 Kelley Wingate Publications   24   KW 1201

Answer Key

113

Name _____ Skill: Sentence Endings

Every sentence has a beginning and an end.

Write the ending of the sentence on the line.

is Spot.
wags.
is brown and black.
play every day.
are big and floppy.

1. My puppy **is brown and black.**

2. His name **is Spot.**

3. His tail always **wags.**

4. His ears **are big and floppy.**

5. We **play every day.**

25 KW 1201

Name _____ Skill: Sentence Endings

Every sentence has a beginning and an end.

Write the ending of the sentence on the line.

make a good dinner.
come out of eggs.
makes a nest.
cry for food.
is in a tree.

1. Mother bird **makes a nest.**

2. The nest **is in a tree.**

3. Baby birds **come out of eggs.**

4. They **cry for food.**

5. Worms **make a good dinner.**

26 KW 1201

Name _____ Skill: Sentence Endings

Every sentence has a beginning and an end.

Write the ending of the sentence on the line.

climb trees.
eat peanuts.
are at the zoo.
roar.
live here.

1. We **are at the zoo.**

2. The monkeys **climb trees.**

3. The lions **roar.**

4. The elephants **eat peanuts.**

5. Many animals **live here.**

27 KW 1201

Name _____ Skill: Sentence Endings

Every sentence has a beginning and an end.

Write the ending of the sentence on the line.

goes on my head.
will be warm.
go on my feet.
is cold outside.
go on my hands.

1. It **is cold outside.**

2. Boots **go on my feet.**

3. Mittens **go on my hands.**

4. A hat **goes on my head.**

5. I **will be warm.**

28 KW 1201

Page 29

Name _____ Skill: Sentence Endings

| Every sentence has a beginning and an end. |

Write the ending of the sentence on the line.

| rolls out the door. |
| calls his kitten. |
| is time to rest. |
| play ball together. |
| comes to him. |

1. Dan _calls his kitten._

2. The kitten _comes to him._

3. Dan and his kitten _play ball together._

4. The ball _rolls out the door._

5. It _is time to rest._

©1996 Kelley Wingate Publications   29   KW 1201

Page 30

Name _____ Skill: Jumbled Sentences

Unscramble the words to make a sentence. Draw a picture about each sentence.

1	2
brown is dog My	dog My barks
My dog is brown.	My dog barks.

3	4
ball plays He	dog My plays me with
He plays ball.	My dog plays with me.

©1996 Kelley Wingate Publications   30   KW 1201

Page 31

Name _____ Skill: Jumbled Sentences

Unscramble the words to make a sentence. Draw a picture about each sentence.

1	2
funny She hat a has	green It is
She has a funny hat.	It is green.

3	4
will a ride horse Father	brown horse The is
Father will ride a horse.	The horse is brown.

©1996 Kelley Wingate Publications   31   KW 1201

Page 32

Name _____ Skill: Jumbled Sentences

Unscramble the words to make a sentence. Draw a picture about each sentence.

1	2
see I kittens three	The asleep are kittens
I see three kittens.	The kittens are asleep.

3	4
me Show bike your	race I bike my
Show me your bike.	I race my bike.

©1996 Kelley Wingate Publications   32   KW 1201

Answer Key

Name _____ Skill: Jumbled Sentences

Unscramble the words to make a sentence. Draw a picture about each sentence.

1 made cake a Mother

Mother made a cake.

2 was The pretty cake

The cake was pretty.

3 jumped frog The

The frog jumped

4 was in It water the

I was in the water.

33 KW 1201

Name _____ Skill: Jumbled Sentences

Unscramble the words to make a sentence. Draw a picture about each sentence.

1 goes car fast This

This car goes fast.

2 It green a car is

It is a green car.

3 climb I tree the

I climb the tree.

4 orange has leaves It

It has orange leaves.

34 KW 1201

Name _____ Skill: Jumbled Sentences

Unscramble the words to make a sentence. Draw a picture about each sentence.

1 have We school at fun

We have fun at school.

2 to like I swing

I like to swing.

3 reads book The a girl

The girl reads a book

4 book The big is

The book is big.

35 KW 1201

Name _____ Skill: Jumbled Sentences

Unscramble the words to make a sentence. Draw a picture about each sentence.

1 away pig One ran

One pig ran away.

2 gate open The was

The gate was open.

3 drink milk We chocolate

We drink chocolate milk.

4 milk us Cows give.

Cows give us milk.

36 KW 1201

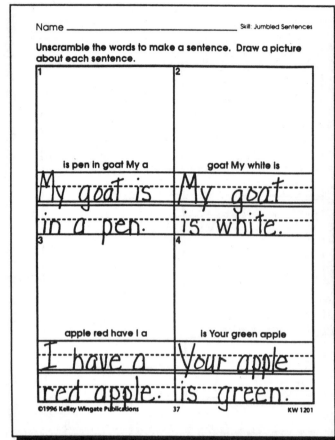

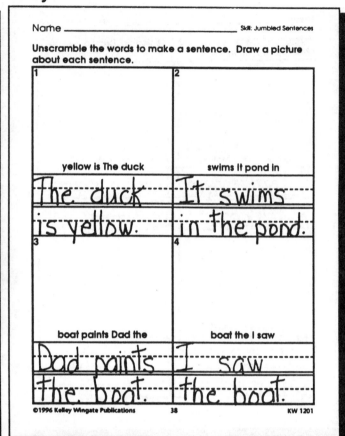

Name _____   Skill: Jumbled Sentences

Unscramble the words to make a sentence. Draw a picture about each sentence.

1	2
Come party my to	play We games will
Come to my party.	We will play games.
3 can run I fast	4 won I ribbon a
I can run fast.	I won a ribbon.

©1996 Kelley Wingate Publications   39   KW 1201

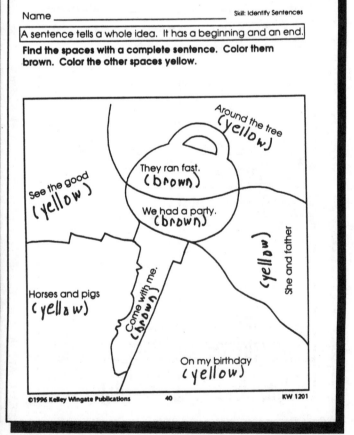

Answer Key

Name _____   Skill: Identify Sentences

A sentence tells a whole idea. It has a beginning and an end.

Find the spaces with a complete sentence. Color them red.
Color the other spaces green.

Take my.
(green)

He has some cake.
(red)

They are.
(green)

(green)

See the red bike.
(red)

This is.

Children jump rope.
(red)

Little blue.
(green)

My big sister.
(green)

with his.
(green)

I am glad
(red)

His yellow boat.
(green)

©1996 Kelley Wingate Publications   41   KW 1201

Name _____   Skill: Identify Sentences

A sentence tells a whole idea. It has a beginning and an end.

Find the spaces with a complete sentence. Color them
green. Color the other spaces orange.

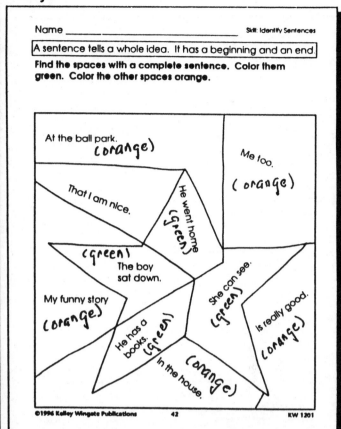

At the ball park.
(orange)

Me too.
(orange)

That I am nice.

He went home
(green)

(green)

The boy
sat down.

My funny story
(orange)

She can see.
(green)

Is really good.
(orange)

He has a
books.
(green)

In the house.
(orange)

(orange)

©1996 Kelley Wingate Publications   42   KW 1201

Name _____   Skill: Identify Sentences

A sentence tells a whole idea. It has a beginning and an end.

Find the spaces with a complete sentence. Color them
yellow. Color the other spaces black.

(black)

Some girls.
(black)

From the barn.

He went away.
(yellow)

He is my friend.
(yellow)

One of you.
(black)

All her toys.
(black)

We like to play.
(yellow)

(black)

Into bed.

I can do it.
(yellow)

My name is.

©1996 Kelley Wingate Publications   43   KW 1201

Name _____   Skill: Identify Sentences

A sentence tells a whole idea. It has a beginning and an end.

Find the spaces with a complete sentence. Color them red.
Color the other spaces purple.

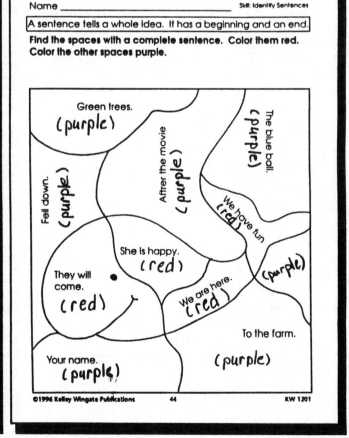

Green trees.
(purple)

The blue ball.
(purple)

After the movie
(purple)

Fell down.
(purple)

We have fun
(red)

She is happy.
(red)

They will
come.
(red)

We are here.
(red)

(purple)

To the farm.

Your name.
(purple)

(purple)

©1996 Kelley Wingate Publications   44   KW 1201

Answer Key

Name _____   Skill: Complete Sentences

A sentence tells a whole idea. It has a beginning and an end.

Write a sentence about each picture. Make the first letter a capital. End with a period. Color the picture.

1. balloon — Sentences will vary.
2. corn
3. milk
4. paper

Name _____   Skill: Complete Sentences

A sentence tells a whole idea. It has a beginning and an end.

Write a sentence about each picture. Make the first letter a capital. End with a period. Color the picture.

1. mitten — Sentences will vary.
2. sun
3. pig
4. baby

Name _____   Skill: Complete Sentences

A sentence tells a whole idea. It has a beginning and an end.

Write a sentence about each picture. Make the first letter a capital. End with a period. Color the picture.

1. leaf — Sentences will vary.
2. kite
3. boat
4. frog

Name _____   Skill: Complete Sentences

A sentence tells a whole idea. It has a beginning and an end.

Write a sentence about each picture. Make the first letter a capital. End with a period. Color the picture.

1. ball — Sentences will vary.
2. cup
3. bee
4. coat

Answer Key

Name _____ Skill: Complete Sentences

A sentence tells a whole idea. It has a beginning and an end.

Write a sentence about each picture. Make the first letter a capital. End with a period. Color the picture.

1. bird — *Sentences will vary.*
2. flower
3. train
4. window

Name _____ Skill: Complete Sentences

A sentence tells a whole idea. It has a beginning and an end.

Write a sentence about each picture. Make the first letter a capital. End with a period. Color the picture.

1. truck — *Sentences will vary.*
2. box
3. fish
4. turtle

Name _____ Skill: Complete Sentences

A sentence tells a whole idea. It has a beginning and an end.

Write a sentence about each picture. Make the first letter a capital. End with a period. Color the picture.

1. car — *Sentences will vary.*
2. bear
3. sock
4. duck

Name _____ Skill: Complete Sentences

A sentence tells a whole idea. It has a beginning and an end.

Write a sentence about each picture. Make the first letter a capital. End with a period. Color the picture.

1. rabbit — *Sentences will vary.*
2. egg
3. shoe
4. goat

Name _____

A sentence tells a whole idea. It has a beginning and an end.

Write a sentence about each picture. Make the first letter a capital. End with a period. Color the picture.

1. farm

2. dress

3. clown

4. fire

Sentences will vary.

Name _____

A sentence tells a whole idea. It has a beginning and an end.

Write a sentence about each picture. Make the first letter a capital. End with a period. Color the picture.

1. mail

2. dog

3. snake

4. cat

Sentences will vary.

Name _____

A sentence that tells us something is called a statement. A statement ends with a period.

Write two statements about each picture. Remember to use capitals and periods.

Statements will vary.

Name _____

A sentence that tells us something is called a statement. A statement ends with a period.

Write two statements about each picture. Remember to use capitals and periods.

Statements will vary.

Name _____   Skill: Writing Statements

A sentence that tells us something is called a statement.
A statement ends with a period.

Write two statements about each picture. Remember to use capitals and periods.

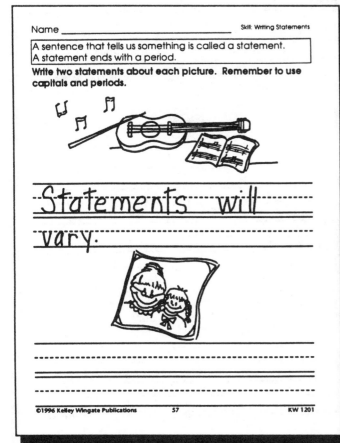

Statements will
vary.

Name _____   Skill: Writing Statements

A sentence that tells us something is called a statement.
A statement ends with a period.

Write two statements about each picture. Remember to use capitals and periods.

Statements will
vary.

Name _____   Skill: Writing Statements

A sentence that tells us something is called a statement.
A statement ends with a period.

Write two statements about each picture. Remember to use capitals and periods.

Statements will
vary.

Name _____   Skill: Writing Statements

A sentence that tells us something is called a statement.
A statement ends with a period.

Write two statements about each picture. Remember to use capitals and periods.

Statements will
vary.

Name _____   Skill: Writing Statements

A sentence that tells us something is called a statement.
A statement ends with a period.

Write two statements about each picture. Remember to use capitals and periods.

Statements will vary.

©1996 Kelley Wingate Publications   61   KW 1201

Name _____   Skill: Writing Statements

A sentence that tells us something is called a statement.
A statement ends with a period.

Write two statements about each picture. Remember to use capitals and periods.

Statements will vary.

©1996 Kelley Wingate Publications   62   KW 1201

Name _____   Skill: Writing Statements

A sentence that tells us something is called a statement.
A statement ends with a period.

Write two statements about each picture. Remember to use capitals and periods.

Statements will vary.

©1996 Kelley Wingate Publications   63   KW 1201

Name _____   Skill: Writing Statements

A sentence that tells us something is called a statement.
A statement ends with a period.

Write two statements about each picture. Remember to use capitals and periods.

Statements will vary.

©1996 Kelley Wingate Publications   64   KW 1201

Answer Key

Worksheet 1 (page 65)

Name _____ Skill: Jumbled Questiions

Unscramble the words to make a question. Draw a picture about each question.

1. Are friend my you
Are you my friend?

2. like you Do school
Do you like school?

3. name is What your
What is your name?

4. wants Who to song a sing
Who wants to sing a song?

© 1996 Kelley Wingate Publications   65   KW 1204

Worksheet 2 (page 66)

Name _____ Skill: Jumbled Questiions

Unscramble the words to make a question. Draw a picture about each question.

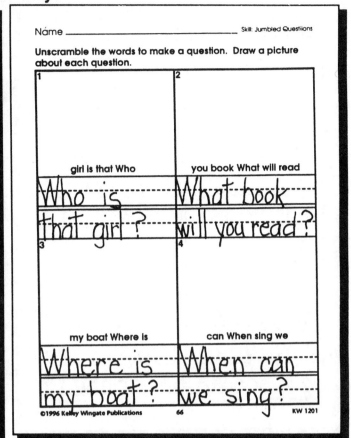

1. girl is that Who
Who is that girl?

2. you book What will read
What book will you read?

3. my boat Where is
Where is my boat?

4. can When sing we
When can we sing?

©1996 Kelley Wingate Publications   66   KW 1201

Worksheet 3 (page 67)

Name _____ Skill: Jumbled Questiions

Unscramble the words to make a question. Draw a picture about each question.

1. blue sky Why the is
Why is the sky blue?

2. How you old are
How old are you?

3. that is ball your
Is that your ball?

4. high Can jump she
Can she jump high?

©1996 Kelley Wingate Publications   67   KW 1201

Worksheet 4 (page 68)

Name _____ Skill: Jumbled Questiions

Unscramble the words to make a question. Draw a picture about each question.

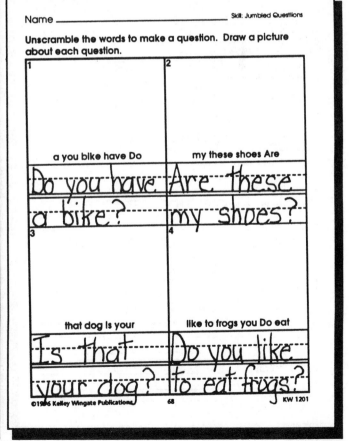

1. a you bike have Do
Do you have a bike?

2. my these shoes Are
Are these my shoes?

3. that dog is your
Is that your dog?

4. like to frogs you Do eat
Do you like to eat frogs?

©1996 Kelley Wingate Publications   68   KW 1201

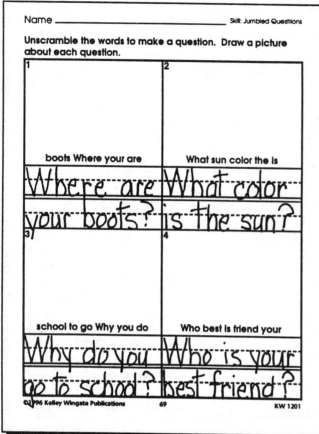

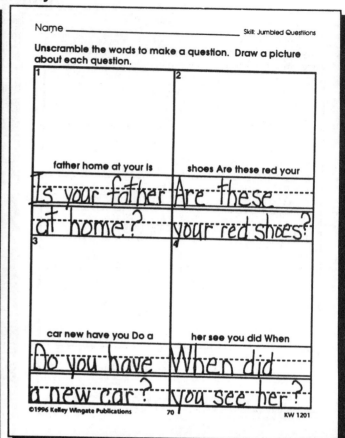

Name _____   Skill: Jumbled Questions

Unscramble the words to make a question. Draw a picture about each question.

1 boots Where your are

Where are your boots?

2 What sun color the is

What color is the sun?

3 school to go Why you do

Why do you go to school?

4 Who best is friend your

Who is your best friend?

©1996 Kelley Wingate Publications   69   KW 1201

Name _____   Skill: Jumbled Questions

Unscramble the words to make a question. Draw a picture about each question.

1 father home at your is

Is your father at home?

2 shoes Are these red your

Are these your red shoes?

3 car new have you Do a

Do you have a new car?

4 her see you did When

When did you see her?

©1996 Kelley Wingate Publications   70   KW 1201

Name _____   Skill: Writing Questions

An asking sentence is a question. It ends with a question mark. Who, what, when, where, why, and how are some words that questions begin with.

Write a question about each picture. Remember to use capitals and question marks.

1. rocket

Questions will vary.

2. skates

3. seal

4. snake

©1996 Kelley Wingate Publications   71   KW 1201

Name _____   Skill: Writing Questions

An asking sentence is a question. It ends with a question mark. Who, what, when, where, why, and how are some words that questions begin with.

Write a question about each picture. Remember to use capitals and question marks.

1. house

Questions will vary.

2. book

3. chicken

4. peas

©1996 Kelley Wingate Publications   72   KW 1201

Answer Key

Name _____

Skill: Writing Questions

An asking sentence is a question. It ends with a question mark. Who, what, when, where, why, and how are some words that questions begin with.

Write a question about each picture. Remember to use capitals and question marks.

1. sign — Questions will vary.
2. glass
3. tent
4. candle

Name _____

Skill: Writing Questions

An asking sentence is a question. It ends with a question mark. Who, what, when, where, why, and how are some words that questions begin with.

Write a question about each picture. Remember to use capitals and question marks.

1. lamp — Questions will vary.
2. sock
3. watch
4. hat

Name _____

Skill: Writing Questions

An asking sentence is a question. It ends with a question mark. Who, what, when, where, why, and how are some words that questions begin with.

Write a question about each picture. Remember to use capitals and question marks.

1. pot — Questions will vary.
2. ring
3. moon
4. teacher

Name _____

Skill: Writing Questions

An asking sentence is a question. It ends with a question mark. Who, what, when, where, why, and how are some words that questions begin with.

Write a question about each picture. Remember to use capitals and question marks.

1. king — Questions will vary.
2. cake
3. jar
4. table

Sheet 1 (top left)

Name _____ Skill: Writing Questions

An asking sentence is a question. It ends with a question mark. Who, what, when, where, why, and how are some words that questions begin with.

Write a question about each picture. Remember to use capitals and question marks.

1. mop — *Questions will vary.*
2. wagon
3. sled
4. plant

©1996 Kelley Wingate Publications   77   KW 1201

Sheet 2 (top right)

Name _____ Skill: Writing Questions

An asking sentence is a question. It ends with a question mark. Who, what, when, where, why, and how are some words that questions begin with.

Write a question about each picture. Remember to use capitals and question marks.

1. bus — *Questions will vary.*
2. star
3. duck
4. coat

©1996 Kelley Wingate Publications   78   KW 1201

Sheet 3 (bottom left)

Name _____ Skill: Writing Questions

An asking sentence is a question. It ends with a question mark. Who, what, when, where, why, and how are some words that questions begin with.

Write a question about each picture. Remember to use capitals and question marks.

1. doll — *Questions will vary.*
2. tree
3. heart
4. horn

©1996 Kelley Wingate Publications   79   KW 1201

Sheet 4 (bottom right)

Name _____ Skill: Writing Questions

An asking sentence is a question. It ends with a question mark. Who, what, when, where, why, and how are some words that questions begin with.

Write a question about each picture. Remember to use capitals and question marks.

1. pool — *Questions will vary.*
2. rain
3. hammer
4. clouds

©1996 Kelley Wingate Publications   80   KW 1201

Name _____   Skill: Writing Stories

These mixed up sentences tell a story. Write the sentences in order on the lines below. Remember to use capitals and periods. Draw a picture for the story.

Making a Cake

1. She put the pan into the oven.

2. Ellen mixed the cake batter.

3. Ellen ate a big piece of the cake.

1. Ellen mixed the cake batter.

2. She put the pan into the oven.

3. Ellen ate a big piece of the cake.

©1996 Kelley Wingate Publications   81   KW 1201

Name _____   Skill: Writing Stories

These mixed up sentences tell a story. Write the sentences in order on the lines below. Remember to use capitals and periods. Draw a picture for the story.

Doing Laundry

1. You then fold the clothes neatly.

2. First, you wash the clothes.

3. Last, you put the clothes away.

1. First, you wash the clothes.

2. You then fold the clothes neatly.

3. Last, you put the clothes away.

©1996 Kelley Wingate Publications   82   KW 1201

Name _____   Skill: Writing Stories

These mixed up sentences tell a story. Write the sentences in order on the lines below. Remember to use capitals and periods. Draw a picture for the story.

Get Ready!

1. Jose went to school.

2. He ate a good breakfast.

3. Jose jumped out of bed.

1. Jose jumped out of bed.

2. He ate a good breakfast.

3. Jose went to school.

©1996 Kelley Wingate Publications   83   KW 1201

Name _____   Skill: Writing Stories

These mixed up sentences tell a story. Write the sentences in order on the lines below. Remember to use capitals and periods. Draw a picture for the story.

Painting

1. Meyer took out paper and paint.

2. Meyer gave the picture to his mother.

3. He painted a pretty picture of a flower.

1. Meyer took out paper and paint.

2. He painted a pretty picture of a flower.

3. Meyer gave the picture to his mother.

©1996 Kelley Wingate Publications   84   KW 1201

Page 85

Name _____

These mixed up sentences tell a story. Write the sentences in order on the lines below. Remember to use capitals and periods. Draw a picture for the story.

The Rabbit

1. The rabbit hopped down a hole near the bush.

2. A rabbit sat under a bush in my yard.

3. I tried to catch the rabbit.

1. A rabbit sat under a bush in my yard.
2. I tried to catch the rabbit.
3. The rabbit hopped down a hole near the bush.

Page 86

Name _____

Write a story about the picture. Use the words in the word box. Remember to begin each sentence with a capital letter and to end it with a period or question mark.

Word Box
puppy
black
lost
home

This black puppy was lost. My mom found him. Now he has a home.

Page 87

Name _____

Write a story about the picture. Use the words in the word box. Remember to begin each sentence with a capital letter and to end it with a period or question mark.

Word Box
ball
throw
high
catch

Stories will vary.

Page 88

Name _____

Write a story about the picture. Use the words in the word box. Remember to begin each sentence with a capital letter and to end it with a period or question mark.

Word Box
beach
pail
water
sand

Stories will vary.

Worksheet (page 89)

Name _____   Skill: Writing Stories

Write a story about the picture. Use the words in the word box. Remember to begin each sentence with a capital letter and to end it with a period or question mark.

Word Box
plane
fly
high
clouds

Stories will vary.

Worksheet (page 90)

Name _____   Skill: Writing Stories

Write a story about the picture. Use the words in the word box. Remember to begin each sentence with a capital letter and to end it with a period or question mark.

Word Box
squirrel
brown
nuts
winter

Stories will vary.

Worksheet (page 91)

Name _____   Skill: Writing Stories

Write a story about the picture. Use the words in the word box. Remember to begin each sentence with a capital letter and to end it with a period or question mark.

Word Box
gray
elephant
trunk
peanuts

Stories will vary.

Worksheet (page 92)

Name _____   Skill: Writing Stories

Write a story about the picture. Use the words in the word box. Remember to begin each sentence with a capital letter and to end it with a period or question mark.

Word Box
petals
flower
yellow
bee

Stories will vary.

Page 93

Skill: Writing Stories

Write a story about the picture. Use the words in the word box. Remember to begin each sentence with a capital letter and to end it with a period or question mark.

Word Box
hide
game
friends
count

Stories will vary.

©1996 Kelley Wingate Publications   93   KW 1201

Page 94

Name _____
Skill: Writing Stories

Write a story about the picture. Use the words in the word box. Remember to begin each sentence with a capital letter and to end it with a period or question mark.

Word Box
storm
clouds
rain
wet

Stories will vary.

©1996 Kelley Wingate Publications   94   KW 1201

Page 95

Name _____
Skill: Writing Stories

Write a story about the picture. Use the words in the word box. Remember to begin each sentence with a capital letter and to end it with a period or question mark.

Word Box
seal
water
ball
swim

Stories will vary.

©1996 Kelley Wingate Publications   95   KW 1201

Page 96

Name _____
Skill: Writing Stories

Write three more words about the picture in the word box. Use the words to write a story about the picture. Remember to begin each sentence with a capital letter.

Word Box
paint
flower
boy
table
(Words will vary)

Stories will vary.

©1996 Kelley Wingate Publications   96   KW 1201

Name _____

Write three more words about the picture in the word box.
Use the words to write a story about the picture. Remember
to begin each sentence with a capital letter.

Word Box
kite
windy
fun
clouds

(Words will vary)

Stories will vary.

Name _____

Write three more words about the picture in the word box.
Use the words to write a story about the picture. Remember
to begin each sentence with a capital letter.

Word Box
bake
flour
milk
sugar

(Words will vary)

Stories will vary.

Name _____

Write three more words about the picture in the word box.
Use the words to write a story about the picture. Remember
to begin each sentence with a capital letter.

Word Box
music
dance
sing
girl

(Words will vary)

Stories will vary.

Name _____

Write three more words about the picture in the word box.
Use the words to write a story about the picture. Remember
to begin each sentence with a capital letter.

Word Box
swim
fish
tank
water

(Words will vary)

Stories will vary.

Page 101

Name _____ Skill: Writing Stories

Write three more words about the picture in the word box.
Use the words to write a story about the picture. Remember
to begin each sentence with a capital letter.

Word Box
chicken
nest
eggs
yellow

(Words will vary)

Stories will vary.

©1996 Kelley Wingate Publications   101   KW 1201

Page 102

Name _____ Skill: Writing Stories

Write three more words about the picture in the word box.
Use the words to write a story about the picture. Remember
to begin each sentence with a capital letter.

Word Box
asleep
bed
dream
pillow

(Words will vary)

Stories will vary.

©1996 Kelley Wingate Publications   102   KW 1201

Page 103

Name _____ Skill: Writing Stories

Write three more words about the picture in the word box.
Use the words to write a story about the picture. Remember
to begin each sentence with a capital letter.

Word Box
ball
puppy
run
roll

(Words will vary)

Stories will vary.

©1996 Kelley Wingate Publications   103   KW 1201

Page 104

Name _____ Skill: Writing Stories

Write three more words about the picture in the word box.
Use the words to write a story about the picture. Remember
to begin each sentence with a capital letter.

Word Box
bus
children
school
yellow

(Words will vary)

Stories will vary.

©1996 Kelley Wingate Publications   104   KW 1201

Certificate of Completion

This certificate certifies that

Has completed

_____

Signed

_____

Date

You Did It!

earns this award for _____

Keep Up The Great Work!

Signed _____

Date _____

CD-3716

Great Success!

_____ earns this award for

_____

I am Proud of You!

_____
Signed

_____
Date

CD-3716

Great Job!

Receives this award for

_____

Keep up the great work!

_____
Signed

_____
Date

CD-3716

Congratulations!

Receives this award for

Keep up the great work!

Signed _____

Date _____

CD-3716

Great Success!

earns this award for

I am Proud of You!

Signed

Date

CD-3716

always	animal	April	away
basket	bear	bed	bike
blow	both	brown	carrot
catch	chair	children	circus

clock	cloud	December	dinner
dinosaur	dollar	eat	egg
elephant	fairy	February	feet
fence	fire	firemen	four

grow	goes	garden	game
have	hard	happy	grass
January	hot dog	horse	honey
king	kick	jar	June

lamb	ladder	know	kite
May	March	love	long
nest	morning	money	milk
owl	October	November	night

prize	sail	shoe	sniff
popcorn	ride	shine	smile
pond	question	September	slow
period	purr	sentence	sister

summer	street	stories	star
trip	trick	tail	table
when	were	wears	water
write	window	wind	where